The Lamplit Answer

The Lamplit Answer

GJERTRUD SCHNACKENBERG

HUTCHINSON

London Melbourne Auckland Johannesburg

First published in Great Britain in 1986
by Century Hutchinson Ltd, Brookmount House,
62-65 Chandos Place, Covent Garden,
London WC2N 4NW

Century Hutchinson Publishing Group (Australia) Pty Ltd
16-22 Church Street, Hawthorn, Melbourne, Victoria 3122

Century Hutchinson (NZ) Ltd
32-34 View Road, PO Box 40-086, Glenfield, Auckland 10

Century Hutchinson Group (SA) Pty Ltd
PO Box 337, Bergvlei 2012, South Africa

Printed and bound in Great Britain by Anchor Brendon Ltd,
Tiptree, Essex

ISBN 0 09 163961 1

Contents

I
———

II
———

III
———

IV
———

I

KREMLIN OF SMOKE

Chopin in the Faubourg Saint-Germain. Winter 1831

1 . The Salon

The swan's neck of the teacup, her black vizard
Plunged underwing, conceals her face like a modest cocotte
Who can't bring herself to look up at the honored guest,
As the silver hammer of the tea service practices
Chings in runs of triplets, and the tea steam hangs
Phantom chrysanthemums on long, evaporating stems
In the air of the winter apartment. The guests,
Having gathered for games, for mimicries,
For gossip's intricate, expensive inventions,
Crowd toward the pianist who, leaning forward,
Clasps his hands, like a child's prison for butterflies,
To begin a tale, perfected in his room, of his
Reception on a tour in the South, where they had hired
A sedan chair with servants to bear him to the theater,
"Like a captured king from a remote, Saxon metropolis,"
And then killed him in the reviews—a smashing joke,
And his hostess snaps her fan shut when she laughs,
In the city of slaves to mirrors, of rivalries
Championed for less than a day by charlatans,
Of politics lending heat to the rented rooms
Of exiled virtuosos, and of cholera warnings affixed
To the posts of the streetlamps, whose heads
Flare with fever from here to the outermost districts.

3

2. *Warsaw, 1820*

The year of childhood's sickbed strewn with novels,
His mother being addicted to the romances
Of Rousseau, although she called them packs of lies,
When four-o'clock's dim lamps beatified
With crimson gilt the borders of the pears
And crescent cakes she brought to usher in
The time she set aside to waste with him
In blissful episodes of idle talk,
Each day, during his fortnight's influenza,
They shuffled cards in slow-collapsing bridges,
And dealt out suits like secret city factions
Whose spreading fans could hide conspiracies
For dealing heavy blows to czars at teatime.
And once, the household clocks passing the news
Of "Five" from room to room, when she stood up
To put away the cards and cold tea,
He, wishing he could keep her there with him,
Thought to detain her with interrogations
And, sinking back to watch the rushing heights
Of falling snow beyond the window glass,
Began by asking her, Where is the snow from?

3. The Salon

And overarching the cream cakes, the pale-skinned meringues,
And the candied violets arranged among the bibelots of the old
Legitimist Bourbons, the pipes and cigars of bespectacled
Millionaire guests fling a kremlin of smoke overhead,
Dome upon dome, rising up to the mauve-tinted heaven
Of trompe-l'oeil clouds, as Chopin, stolen from
The *Comédie* by the piano gods, with a tablecloth over
His shoulders, enacts "My Viennese Laundress." He points
To the imaginary trays of the French sausagemaker's
Shop-window display, and quavers in an indignant contralto,
"Ach! Those sausages were ground from dogs und alley cats,
Mein Herr, und the remains of guillotined aristocrats!"
Dome upon dome, from which orders issue to plunder
His childhood home, while here the hostess lifts her hand,
At which high-sign the grand piano is rolled in,
Its curving wing unfolded, like a great black butterfly
That slowly sails toward charades by candlelight
Across the polished chasm of parquet.

4. *Warsaw, 1820*

He thought she hadn't heard him, seeing how
She stopped, as if enchanted, hands outstretched
And frozen half in flight above the cards,
Her profile turned three-quarters toward the glass,
A statue stolen from last summer's game
Of Statues, when his great-aunt's hand composed
The winning title for his mother's pose
As "Time, caught in the act of listening
Outside the walls of music." Then he heard it,
The dreaded, spectral carriages of thunder
Rolling toward their house, like the Grand Duke
—Pavlovich!—coming to fetch the prodigy
In an amusing, minor act of war:
Subjection in the form of flattery
Heaped on the Polish people's little star
Scavenged from Warsaw's cultural debris,
A star still at the age whose wishbones bleach,
Forgotten, in the dining-room armoire,
The age of funerals held for nightingales.
But then, when she resumed her task again,
She answered neither, What? nor, I don't know.
Rather, turning her profile from the glass
That cut in half a slowly building drift
Like the cross-section of an empty palace,
She answered him, The snow—it comes from Moscow.

5. Chopin's Apartment

His irritation at the threshold's creak
Beneath the servant's foot this afternoon
Had seemed rather enacted than experienced,
His petulant rebuke, the spectacle
In which it seemed he played it to the hilt,
An exiled Master flown into a passion
Who'd fled a nine-year-old's piano lesson
To lock himself upstairs into his room.
And while his scolded pupil's lowered face
In silhouette above the keyboard wore
His reprimand in prisms on her lashes,
A sylph staring, up close, into a pearl—
The glamour of vain outbursts lost on her,
The sweeping gesture of his obstinate
Refusal, even now, to come downstairs!—
A tantrum nearly comical, except
His struggle to restrain his brimming tears
And effort to choke back his wish to blame
Her threw him back onto his couch
Forceful as if self-pity could foreguess
How, from the fourth-floor window of a house
In Warsaw occupied by Russian soldiers,
The soldiers on a lark have seized and hurled,
As if thunder itself turned visible,
Chopin's piano crashing to the street,
And burned the wreck—though here in fact,
Surrounded by the yards of silk he's hung

Around his room "gray as the river Seine,"
He doesn't know for what it is he cries;
And holds, swimming before his eyes, no image
But his pair of slippers through a heavy blur,
Embroidered slippers propped and motionless,
And, pictured in the blind-stitched calla lily's
White, upwhirling spathe, a burning bridge.

6. The Salon

Bayed in the lap of the Marchioness, the littlest
And most charming monkey in Paris, who appears
To have crossed childhood's threshold middle-aged,
Murders a lily, wringing it by the stem,
Then flings it aside as the recital begins,
And the powder shaken from the lily's horn
Scatters like crumbs of fire across the floor,
As a Nocturne, circling the room, floats out
Above the sidewalks of the faubourg among
The snow-bound lanterns, whose dimmed flames
Smolder behind their framed, white squares of snow
That verge on disintegration—as a page,
Ignited on the grate and now gone cold,
Maintains its structure as a work of ash
Whose letters breathe like ghosts of butterflies
Barely respiring, and legible unless
Gloved fingertips should touch them curiously
And make them crumble: "You are a Russian, God!"
Upstairs applause breaks out like muffled war,
And on the street a dozen men have ceased
To knock the heaps of snow to fragile flocks,
But fling aside their shovels to applaud.

7. Warsaw, 1822

There the beloved pelican, dressed in a shredded frock coat,
With a purplish nose and the lavender, lopsided wig
Got at a steal from King Stanislav's auctioned-off wardrobe,
Would, mid-lesson, the better to emphasize his points,
Arise into a carpet-slipper quadrille and wave
His stick in lightning shapes before the boy
Already proclaimed the Russian nobles' darling,
Admonishing: Now! Thunder away like mad! Think big!
The professor who, at the close of their final lesson,
Had counted off on his once-famous fingers
The five things every pianist must remember:

One, to ignore the unthinkable folly of Weber;
Two, to ignore every so-called Italian composer;
Three, to ignore the conventions surrounding one's need
For a bath, since a rubdown with vodka will do;
Four, to ignore, all respect, Ludwig Beethoven—too cataclysmic;
Five, most important, this last being saved for the thumb,
To ignore where you are and whomever it is you perform for:
"Larks, for example—what do they care who deposes
The King of all Poland? I needn't say I refer
To the Viceroy, may he and his uncles and aunts
And his furthest descendants, however remote, burn
Forever—but the larks will give tongue to a phrase
Neither Polish nor Russian, and do so as freely
From the branches of trees in the private park
Of the archfiend as in your mother's kitchen-garden, son.

And what are their motives for singing?"—turning his hand
Slowly over to empty out nothing—"Precisely none."

8. Chopin's Journal

Once I have grasped it, a fever comes out
Hanging lanterns on the wide staircases,
One by one, leading to the courtyard where,
Though I advocate nothing, still my eyes
Detect within the eyes of my companion
The imperceptible paranoia of the charlatan,
Like hummingbirds taking sugar-water sips,
Flickering scarlet tints in his irises.
So the topic is flowers, and proposing to contemplate
Their aristocratic deaths, I say, "In Poland
We say the crown is reached only through
The imagination," as from a silver tray
Of showy blossoms I choose one to twirl
By its stem: a creamy camellia, ruffled
As the hem of the Marquise's gown, through which
The maid's heavy iron slowly drifted
That she may longer twirl and twirl beneath
The arbor where lilacs foam along
The crest of the waltz craze, though the first
Mottles of corruption edge the petals,
Like the tarnish on the scissors which
Decapitated it. Flowers, because
I too am an outcome withering from my cause.

THE SELF-PORTRAIT OF
IVAN GENERALIĆ

The school of naïve painters, Hlebine, Yugoslavia. Oil on glass, 1975

Once distant villages hung in the trees
Like God the Father's stars, and pigs transformed
The grass with wedding feasts, and goslings swarmed

Running like kindergarteners from the geese,
Glad in the farmyards of the sacred heart,
The windows of the Lord where sunsets brimmed

Around the heads of sheep, as gold-leaf rimmed
The gospel pages where we played a part
Until God chased you crying from the world:

There we were saved. Lambs stepped on skinny legs
To baby-sit the hidden, fragile eggs
When birds, flown to the Crucifixion, swirled

And snapped the fresh white linen in their beaks,
Draping the shroud of Jesus in the yard.
But now I take it back, I take it hard,

I take it up with Him whose evening streaks
The violet flash of Christ beyond the fence,
As tears make purple clouds of Bible ink

On gospel leaves of onionskin. I think
Of roots touching your face in ignorance.
Once onions curled like gospels from your knife,

Once roosters spread their wings like Christ entombed
But risen, stepping through the stony room
The way foals rise and wobble into life

Before their mothers' eyes. I take it back.
Instead our windows darken into squares
Of night, from which you've vanished, window squares

Like Bibles closed forever, squares of black.

SIGNS

Threading the palm, a web of little lines
Spells out the lost money, the heart, the head,
The wagging tongues, the sudden deaths, in signs
We would smooth out, like imprints on a bed,

In signs that can't be helped, geese heading south,
In signs read anxiously, like breath that clouds
A mirror held to a barely open mouth,
Like telegrams, the gathering of crowds—

The plane's X in the sky, spelling disaster:
Before the whistle and hit, a tracer flare;
Before rubble, a hairline crack in plaster
And a housefly's panicked scribbling on the air.

TWO TALES OF CLUMSY

I

When Clumsy harks the gladsome ting-a-lings
Of dinner chimes that Mrs. Clumsy rings,
His two hands winglike at his most bald head,
Then Clumsy readies Clumsy to be fed.
He pulls from satchel huge a tiny chair,
And waggling his pillowed derriere

He hitches up his pants to gently sit.
Like two ecstatic doves his white hands flit
Tucking his bib in quickly, then, all thumbs,
They brush away imaginary crumbs
From knee-high table with dismissive air.
With fists wrapped round his giant silverware

He shuts his eyes and puckers up for kisses.
In such a pose Clumsy awaits his Mrs.,
Rubbing his hungry ribs. But oh, alack,
Quite unbeknownst to Clumsy, at his back
The circle of a second spotlight shows
That No-No has delivered fatal blows

To Mrs. Clumsy since that happy time
She summoned Clumsy with her dinner chime.
And there is Clumsy's darling lying dead.
How like a rubber ball bounces her head
As No-No drags her feet-first from this life.
Then No-No dresses up as Clumsy's wife,

Her scarf now silhouettes his long hooked nose,
His long bones rattle in her frilly clothes
As No-No bears a tray of cups and plates
Into the light where puckered Clumsy waits.
Hearing her footstep soft makes Clumsy take
The pucker from his lips and sweetly break

Into falsetto greetings, then resume
His lips into a kiss. But this is doom,
And hideously silent No-No stands.
When Clumsy parts his eyelids both his hands
Fly up as if on strings and Clumsy screams,
The tears squirt from his ducts a dozen streams,

His mouth blubbers, inelegantly smeared,
"Where is she, No-No? Oh, I am afeared!"
Then No-No lifts up Clumsy's trembly chin,
And leans to hiss with loud stage whisper in
The big pink ear of Clumsy, "My dear friend,"
No-No enunciates, "this is The End."

Disguised as Doctor of Philosophy
In academic haberdashery
By dint of hood and black capacious gown,
No-No wipes off the blackboard up and down,
His black sleeve floating outward with each lunge,
The black streaks glisten from his dampened sponge,

While Clumsy sharpens pencils two feet long
To little stubs and wets them with his tongue,
Then smooths his pad of paper with gloved fists.
He lifts his sleeves a fraction at the wrists
And twirls his hands around like windmill sails
To soothe his nerves, then drums his muffled nails

Until the Doctor claps his hands rat-tat
And picks his pointer up and points it at
His eager pupil with the jumbo ears:
"Compose a paragraph." And Clumsy clears
His throat a dozen times to soft aver,
"I don't know how to write with letters sir."

At which the Doctor hides with sleeve a smile
Most uncontrollable and fraught with guile,
Until, authority regained, he says,
"In that case you may dictate sentences
Which you most wish to write, and I'll record
Your words for you to copy from the board."

Now Clumsy tries to think of what to write.
He cranes his neck around stage-left and -right,
He gazes toward the rafters thinking hard
And sometimes shakes his head as to discard
Ideas he finds less than adequate,
Then caroling a joyous "I know what!"

He pulls a giant light-bulb from a sack
And holds it overhead and puts it back,
And in his vast excitement both his hands
Pull up his earlobe-anchored rubber bands
To lift from scalp his tiny frizzy wig:
"I'd like to start with 'God is very big.' "

Erupting laughter nearly knocks quite down
The Doctor in his nearly empty gown,
He whirls on heel and cuts his hooting off:
"My theologian! Fellow *philosophe*!
Your disquisition bears the resonance
Of truth's unique, unutterable sense

But yet, being pedantic and antique,
This mind of mine must tinker, weigh, and seek,
And wonder if together you and I
For sake of scholarship should specify
How big God is?" Thus groping for the truth
About the size of God makes pink smoke poof

From Clumsy's ears in jets, and fire alarms
Go off backstage as, lowered head on arms,
Full sixty seconds Clumsy cogitates.
The Doctor snaps his chalk in two and waits.
Clumsy looks up and No-No utters "Yes?"
"Bigger than cloud formations, I would guess."

"Bigger than clouds! Dear fellow! I should say
I never would have thought of God that way!
Then let's begin." And No-No sets the chalk
Tick-ticking on the board like time-bomb clock
While Clumsy wraps his pencil finger-wise
And sets it on the page and squints his eyes

At No-No's blackboard words so white and clean
And neat and straight with spaces in between,
And then, his page two inches from his nose,
He copies out in crooked uphill rows:
"I, Clumsy, hereby give and wittingly
My soul to No-No for Eternity."

II

IMAGINARY PRISONS

A version of "Sleeping Beauty." In memory of Colin Way Reid

The gardeners gazing through their open shears
Or staring sightless from their wooden ladders
Stand helpless by and dream they cannot lower

Their upraised sickles poised a hundred years
Above the labyrinth of stems, as briars,
Even while dreaming of their destinies

As smoke and ashes in the gardeners' fires,
Fasten themselves around the spellbound blades
And steal the dreamers' hats in mockery

To lift them out of reach of stick and ladder,
Then lose them on their way to taking over
The twilit walls and roofs and hundred chimneys

Against whose edifices chimney-swallows
Have woven for their families habitations
With rosebud twigs and dust of crumbled mortar

And threads they've tugged gently as milliners
From out the silken shirts and ruffled trousers
Of failed princes hidden in the brambles,

The swallows unaware these men have starved
Entangled in their struggles with the briars.
Yet every year more numerous and scary

These faces one by one among the roses
Bear witness to the private agony
Of what it means to have a single purpose.

Peacocks patrol the garden's sleeping borders
Malicious as a troop of evil fairies
Who pace and lash the brickwork with their feathers'

Opalescent hems, and pacing screech
How perilous is purity of heart.
And briars tentatively hoist their thorns

Across the dizzying ledges schisms form
Where being and non-being break apart.

*

The kitchen boy distracted by a quarrel
Is dreaming that he opens up a box
Of banished knives blinding even at twilight

And this way makes his adversary cower,
But ducks in fact before the furnace-stoker
Around whose lifted shovel embers sparkle

And hang like bumblebees around a flower.
And though you laugh, to them it greatly matters,
For they've had confirmation of the rumor

Touching upon the kitchen maid's betrothal;
The girl whom both of them have tried to capture
Like awkward brooms chasing a wind-borne feather

Today revealed her secret plans to marry
A woodcutter from the adjoining forest
Who's older than both rivals put together,

The only man the girl has wanted ever.
But tell me, seeing how in joy her fingers
Touch her reflection in the plate of copper

It is her task to breathe upon and burnish
As gently as a sleeper barely breathing,
Say who could wish the future on another?

For she must wake from momentary rapture
Into a grief approaching lunacy
To learn, among the skeletons of princes,

A humbler man has long since lost the struggle
And witnessed to the end the work of briars
As, blooming through his slowly loosened fingers,

They carried off his ax as if it were
A weightless toy among the waves of roses.
Upstairs her mistress in a sitting chamber

Has drawn a diamond from a velvet sack
Intending to bequeath it to her daughter,
But transfixed in the dream with palm outstretched

As though to weigh a flame she seems to shiver
In finding that the diamond, howsoever
Its light wobbles unstable as a fire,

Feels to her sightless fingers icy black.

*

The mountain ranges on the moon never
So near as now, never so clear, never
So brilliant with a brimming tenderness

As here before the court astronomer
Who sleeps beguiled at his telescope
And dreams he has beheld the final vision,

Granted after the lifetime he has given
To studying the systems of the night.
He dreams, sunk in a lit, celestial slumber,

That lifting up his eyes he has observed
Beyond the black of night the boundary
And inner surface of the crystal sphere

And curved foundation wall of the sublime
By which we are enclosed, he dreams, with light,
Where black to rushing radiance is transformed

And matter into spirit evanesced.
He dreams his life's not wasted, furthermore,
For all is as his formulas suggest,

The diagrams and models of the worlds
Which he's spent years committing to the care
Of tranquil, pencil-covered papers rest

All in perfect accord with what he sees.
So let him sleep, and sleep enthralled, and never
Mind that it's a false discovery,

And please, don't pipe up that the obstacle
Of blackness which he dreams he's looking through
Is just as black as it was black before,

And fully insurmountable as ever.
For you and I know walls as high or higher,
And each of us has dreamed a private terror,

Or call it whatsoever you desire,
Disintegrates and blows away and clears
Our paths until we waken to discover

The very thing we thought had disappeared
Still waits for us in silence up ahead.
So leave him his perfected universe

Fulfilled as it was promised in his theory,
Leave him the page on which his calipers
Are perched and shining like a triangle

Of light beams springing from his pencil marks.
Leave him, though you and I are taught the sky
Is backed up by a blackness like a hammer

Already fallen on his circular
Irradiated dream as if the spheres
Were balls of glass shattered in jagged angles

Even geometry is dumbstruck by.

*

The seamstress caught up in a dream of sewing
Is dreaming that in lieu of banished scissors
She can't employ to cut an abstract pattern

She can't affix to cloth with banished pins,
Is dreaming that her two hands grip a flowing
Bolt of cloudy, lightning-colored fabric

Which she is poised with all her rapt attention
To tear in one electric flash of noise.
And clowning like a slave of comedy

The aging simpleton whom she has hired
In sympathy is pressing in his fervor
The bonnet top which he elects to wear

To keep the weather off winter and summer,
And dreaming of his job of chasing flies.
Beneath the shadow of his lifted swatter,

The housefly dreams she wrings her hands with worry.
Below this workshop lies the court's despairing
Lone perpetual insomniac,

Alarmed as if he overheard their dreaming.
But seeing how he's grown perversely eager,
Lying flat out and hopeless on his back,

To learn at last which sound will finally shatter
His nerves so thoroughly that it will keep
His body, mind, and soul awake forever,

I'll grant you that it's something of a challenge
To stifle giggles, for, with sheets and covers
Pulled up around his wakeful head adorned

With layered nightcaps like a crown of flannel
With puffy parts for muffling the ears,
He looks like some unheard-of king of cabbage

Condemned forever in his lonely garden
To dreaming that he cannot fall asleep.

*

Assigned to live next door, because he's silent,
Though under lock and key, because he's mad,
The ruler's brother sits with elbows propped

And hands holding his face above the trestle,
Regarding through the prison of his fingers
The specter of an empty china platter

As he's regarded it for countless years
Since he was thunder-stricken to discover
A trivial flaw disastrous to his theory

In which the world is made of porcelain,
But porcelain that cannot crack or shatter
As demonstrated in his published paper,

"The Paradigm of Glass Unbreakable,"
With which he thought to rectify the anger
Of those like him who'd keenly felt the bitter

Accident of being dropped and broken.
And yet the dunderheads refused to hear!
And given that the blind, refining forces

Which glaze the world in an ideal fire
Appeared to have no meaning to the others,
He ceased evangelizing and retired,

Dropping exhausted to his study chair,
And turned to meditation to restore
His faith and to refresh his memory

By summoning the specter of a platter
To represent our wholly perfect order,
And that's the moment, as I said before,

That this unfortunate was struck by thunder
And terrified to see, and no mistaking,
The surface showed the first hint of a fissure,

A web of cracks across the porcelain
Like black lightning unrolled and fixed forever
Into the lightly shattered glaze was creeping,

A test of faith which lengthened year by year
Before his swearing of a vow to stare
Until the fragile web of laws breaking

The tragic glaze apart come to appear
To be the laws by which it's held together.

                                        *

Behind the man trapped in the labyrinths
And mazes of his theory's shattered beauty,
The chimney sweep like an incongruous

And homely soldier standing at attention
Is troubled into a dream of reverence
Since he in the fulfillment of his duty

With savage mop widowed a chimney-swallow
Whose voice, he dreams, still flutes from out of doors
Like a petition for the simplest mercy,

Calling his mate back from a territory
No mapmaker is hired to consider,
One prison engineered within another

And hidden in the blackness of the chimney.
Though you and I are schooled in the motto
That goes, "A stranger's tears are only water,"

Though we hold in the very least regard
The sentiments of such a worthless rascal
As does to death an ordinary swallow,

And though you scoff that having murdered her
The boy is stunned before her crumpled figure,
That he once having seen the swallow fallen,

And with a premonition of disaster,
Is moved to doff his cap and mourn in honor
Of one however small who has crossed over

The line dividing nothingness from history,
If you think "nothingness" goes way too far,
If "history" is the word that sets you crowing

It isn't history if it isn't written—
It's written here, and written here in favor
Of one who's flown ahead of us to enter

That nothing than which there is nothing vaster.

*

The angelfish streaming their whispered letters
Are dreaming they turn back from what they whisper
To flee along their unseen, drifting ladders,

Abandoned in the poet's empty quarters
Since he was carted off a prisoner
And charged, lacking the benefit of lawyers,

With sharpening his pencil to a point
Nearly approaching the invisible.
Absurd, you say, that any could consider

A pencil point a real and present danger,
Yet here he keeps, in the remotest tower,
The company of sundry malefactors

All dressed in jailbird hats and jailbird shirts,
And dreams his angelfish are drawing near
The paper he's spread out across his table,

Like candle flames they flicker as they whisper
The letters he transcribes, and back and forth
Their wobbling reflections through the water

Give to the page an underlight of fire
As if fire were a property of paper.
And drowsing next to him, the king's bird-keeper,

Arrested for importing foreign birds
Sharp-beaked enough to constitute a peril,
Is dreaming that the brass keys of the jailer

Chirp in the locks of manacles and fetters,
Soft as the first in all the aviary
To voice a note before the blackness clears.

Nearby the drunkard dreams of foaming beer,
The counterfeiter dreams of flawless money
That issues from his confiscated needle

In spectral temples, webs, and ghostly scrolls
Blooming in portraitures of shadowed numerals.
Nearby the painter, dragged in by the collar

For spending his allotment for a year's
Supply of paints on one half ounce of umber,
Is dreaming that his new-laid patch of plaster

Is parching dry as desert sand before
He's able to complete his fragmentary
Fresco of utopian waterways

Where dolphin-leaps like transitory doors
To palaces across the water form
Shining parabolas above canals.

*

Here too, wrongly denounced as a false servant
When he foresaw the devastating scandal
Attendant on the infant's christening,

And then arrested on the ruler's orders
When he described the blackness furthermore
Which Beauty at the hour of betrayal

Would see within the light of birthday candles,
The court's clairvoyant dreams that on the stairs
That spiral downward to his darkened parlor

His wife is standing stricken at the door,
Reading the posted writ of his arrest
As if the black-gloved hand of the informer

Were laid directly on her narrow shoulder.
And you and I can see: his dream is true.
Nodding above his handcuffs in the corner,

And exiled from all company, but for
The presence of two mirror-image spiders
Who dream they wage an obscure tournament,

The traitor dreams of climbing up a ladder
Reaching from prison moat to prison tower,
Although a tower less and less familiar,

And dreams, casting his eyes over his shoulder,
He sees the ladder upside down in water,
Himself as he climbs higher growing smaller,

Himself as he looks downward looking upward,
And dreams he scrambles, falls, and crashes toward
His death with outstretched arms, and there

Is met by no one but the water's mirrored
Looming, panicked image of himself.

*

The king's uneasiness at coming trauma
Compels him to the shop of the clockmaker
Where one by one on his more desperate orders

According to his right of search-and-seizure
The kingdom's clocks were hauled in all together
And all of them, like world-is-ending seers

Incarcerated for the way they chatter,
Telling obsessively a single story
Over and over, all reduced the ruler

To telling them, Shut up! Shut up! Shut up!
And now dismantled, emptied, strewn in parts
Across the benches, tables, sills, and floors,

They've fallen silent as their very maker
Who sits with his demolished masterworks
And following instructions slowly lowers

His brush dejected into paint dissolver
To swab away the black of painted numbers
From every clock face in the territory,

The disassembled royal water-chimes,
The cuckoo clocks wearing a look of terror,
The grandfathers dumped out like ransacked drawers,

The microcosmic wheels and golden gears
And useless screws and labyrinths of wires
And miniature bells and gongs and hammers

And swaying springs like just-beheaded roses
And black unfastened dials pointing where
There's nothing left to point at but the ruler

Who with his crown exchanged for the watchmaker's
Headband with the lens extended forward
Is breathless with attention bending over

The timepiece of his father's father's father
Which he is touching with the jeweler's
Diminutive, unaging pair of tweezers

As if to halt once and for all the source
Of seconds, minutes, hours, days, and years.
And this is how we find him, as he stares

Sightless into the ruined factory
Bequeathed to him, and dreams that he discovers
The future isn't manufactured there—

It's manufactured somewhere in the past,
The present in the past, past in the past,
It lies beyond his legislative power

Though banging gavels bring his courts to order
And pound out points of law as sharp or sharper
Than pencils, pins and needles, knives and scissors:

The future in the past is fixed forever,
Like words locked up in pencils, webs in spiders,
Like flames imprisoned in the match tip's sulphur,

Like thorns locked up in seeds hidden in roses
Imprisoned in the budding stems of briars.
He cannot overrule the condemnation:

More patient than a needle in a drawer,
It is the past that lies in wait for her,
Concealing in a point grown ever sharper

The blood drops of the mock assassination—

*

And rightly dreams he cannot save another.
And though you rush to say he rests assured
Of the compassion of the dispensation,

And though the promised torch already burns
By which the briars are lit and roses turn
To smoke and ashes in the gardeners' fires

Through which the true prince walks and is unharmed,
I've learned to make a study of the hour
When grander schemes that mock our calculations

Reveal that we're the emblems standing for
The consequence of what we cannot master.
Say what you wish about the past and future,

But we have learned that here and now is where
All time stops in a face we've held as dear
As she is held who's overcome with roses,

And now is never where the promised fires
Are burning, but the time that's set apart
For you and I to stand and sightless stare,

As gardeners gazing through their open shears
Stand in the shadows of the promised briars.

DARWIN IN 1881

Sleepless as Prospero back in his bedroom
In Milan, with all his miracles
Reduced to sailors' tales,
He sits up in the dark. The islands loom.
His seasickness upwells,
Silence creeps by in memory as it crept
By him on water, while the sailors slept,
From broken eggs and vacant tortoise shells.
His voyage around the cape of middle age
Comes, with a feat of insight, to a close,
The same way Prospero's
Ended before he left the stage
To be led home across the blue-white sea,
When he had spoken of the clouds and globe,
Breaking his wand, and taking off his robe:
Knowledge increases unreality.

He quickly dresses.
Form wavers like his shadow on the stair
As he descends, in need of air
To cure his dizziness,
Down past the ship-sunk emptiness
Of grownup children's rooms and hallways where
The family portraits stare,
All haunted by each other's likenesses.

Outside, the orchard and a piece of moon
Are islands, he an island as he walks,
Brushing against weed stalks.

By hook and plume
The seeds gathering on his trouser legs
Are archipelagoes, like nests he sees
Shadowed in branching, ramifying trees,
Each with unique expressions in its eggs.
Different islands conjure
Different beings; different beings call
From different isles. And after all
His scrutiny of Nature
All he can see
Is how it will grow small, fade, disappear,
A coastline fading from a traveler
Aboard a survey ship. Slowly,
As coasts depart,
Nature had left behind a naturalist
Bound for a place where species don't exist,
Where no emergence has a counterpart.

He's heard from friends
About the other night, the banquet hall
Ringing with bravos—like a curtain call,
He thinks, when the performance ends,
Failing to summon from the wings
An actor who had lost his taste for verse,
Having beheld, in larger theaters,
Much greater banquet vanishings
Without the quaint device and thunderclap
Required in Act 3.
He wrote, Let your indulgence set me free,

To the Academy, and took a nap
Beneath a *London Daily* tent,
Then puttered on his hothouse walk
Watching his orchids beautifully stalk
Their unreturning paths, where each descendant
Is the last—
Their inner staircases
Haunted by vanished insect faces
So tiny, so intolerably vast.
And, while they gave his proxy the award,
He dined in Downe and stayed up rather late
For backgammon with his beloved mate,
Who reads his books and is, quite frankly, bored.

Now, done with beetle jaws and beaks of gulls
And bivalve hinges, now, utterly done,
One miracle remains, and only one.
An ocean swell of sickness rushes, pulls,
He leans against the fence
And lights a cigarette and deeply draws,
Done with fixed laws,
Done with experiments
Within his greenhouse heaven where
His offspring, Frank, for half the afternoon
Played, like an awkward angel, his bassoon
Into the humid air
So he could tell
If sound would make a Venus's-flytrap close.
And, done for good with scientific prose,

That raging hell
Of tortured grammars writhing on their stakes,

He'd turned to his memoirs, chuckling to write
About his boyhood in an upright
Home: a boy preferring gartersnakes
To schoolwork, a lazy, strutting liar
Who quite provoked her aggravated look,
Shushed in the drawing room behind her book,
His bossy sister itching with desire
To tattletale—yes, that was good.
But even then, much like the conjurer
Grown cranky with impatience to abjure
All his gigantic works and livelihood
In order to immerse
Himself in tales where he could be the man
In Once upon a time there was a man,

He'd quite by chance beheld the universe:
A disregarded game of chess
Between two love-dazed heirs
Who fiddle with the tiny pairs
Of statues in their hands, while numberless
Abstract unseen
Combinings on the silent board remain
Unplayed forever when they leave the game
To turn, themselves, into a king and queen.
Now, like the coming day,
Inhaled smoke illuminates his nerves.

He turns, taking the sandwalk as it curves
Back to the yard, the house, the entrance way
Where, not to waken her,

He softly shuts the door,
And leans against it for a spell before
He climbs the stairs, holding the banister,
Up to their room: there
Emma sleeps, moored
In illusion, blown past the storm he conjured
With his book, into a harbor
Where it all comes clear,
Where island beings leap from shape to shape
As to escape
Their terrifying turns to disappear.
He lies down on the quilt,
He lies down like a fabulous-headed
Fossil in a vanished riverbed,
In ocean drifts, in canyon floors, in silt,
In lime, in deepening blue ice,
In cliffs obscured as clouds gather and float;
He lies down in his boots and overcoat,
And shuts his eyes.

III

LOVE LETTER

Dear love, though I'm a hopeless correspondent,
I found your letter habits lacking too
Till I received your card from H.-lulu.
It made me more-than-slightly-less despondent
To see how you transformed your ocean swim
Among dumb bubble-blowers into meters
And daffy rhymes about exotic tweeters
Beyond your balcony at 2 a.m.

I went to bed when you went to Hawaii,
And shut my eyes so tightly I saw stars,
And clenched my sheets like wadded-up memoirs,
And made some noise like wah-wah-wah, i.e.,
I find your absence grimly problematic.
The days stack up like empty boxes stored
In ever-higher towers of cardboard
Swaying in senseless-lost-time's spooky attic.
I'll give the -atic rhyme another try.
To misconstrue the point-of-view Socratic,
Life is a painful stammered-out emphatic
Pronunciation of the word Goodbye.

Or, as it came out on the telephone,
Sooner-the-better is the way I see it:
Just say, "I guess not"; I'll reply, "So be it."
Beloved, if you throw this dog a bone,
To readopt the stray-dog metaphor,
I'll keep my vigil till the cows come home.
You'll hear me howling over there in Rome.

I have no explanations, furthermore—
But let me say I've had it up to here
With scrutinizing the inscrutable;
The whys and how-comes of immutable
Unhesitating passion are unclear—

I don't love you because you're good at rhymes,
And not because I think you're not-so-dumb,
I don't love you because you make me come
And come and come innumerable times,
And not for your romantic overcoats,
And not because our friends all say I should,
And not because we wouldn't or we would
Be or not be at one another's throats,
And not because your accent thrills my ear—
Last night you said not "sever" but "severe,"
But then "severe" describes the act "to sever"—
I love you for no reason whatsoever

And that's the worst, as William S. the Bard
Wrote out in black-and-white while cold-and-hot:
Reasons can be removed, but love cannot.
The comic view insists: Don't take it hard,
But every day I'm pacing up and down
The hallway till I drive my neighbors mad,
And evenings come with what-cannot-be-had
As lights blink on around this boring town,
Whence I unplug the phone and draw the shade
And drink myself half-blind and fantasize

That we're between the sheets, your brilliant eyes
Open on me and, bang, we have it made—
When in reality I sit alone
And, staring at my hands, I think "I think
Till love and fame to nothingness do sink"
While hating everything I've always known
About how you and I are sunk as well.

Under the aspect of eternity
The world already ended anyway.
And, without you, my life can go to hell
On roller skates, as far as I'm concerned.
Two things are clear: these quatrains should be burned,
And love is awful, but it leads us to
Our places in the human comedy,
Frescoes of which abound in Italy,
And though I won't be sitting next to you,
I'll take my seat with minimal complaints.
May you sit in the company of saints
And intellectuals and fabulous beauties,
And not forget this constant love of Trude's.

COMPLAINT

I lean over the rail toward the dark town,
The rail a streak of cloud in piled snow,
The stairs cloud-piled around the balcony.
His house is lit below,

One light among the branches at my feet.
I look, and press my hands into the snow.
I think that I am inconsolable.
No path to him, I know

Of none but that I follow into sleep
To where he waits, I hurry through the snow
To where the man stands waiting in the dream.
He loves, he tells me so,

He kisses me until the ceiling dome
Parts overhead and snow is coming through,
Until heaven itself, empty of snow,
Opens above us too,

His hands melting the snow into my hair
Until I wake. Since he'll not have me, no,
I come out to the balcony and press
My hands into the snow,

And close my eyes, since he is blind to me.
Since he'll not hear me, then I'll be deaf too,
And draw my hair into a set of strings
I'll take a scissors to.

SONATA

Overture

More loudly to inveigh against your absence,
Raising the volume by at least a third,
Humbly I say I've written this immense
Astonishing "Sonata" word by word,
With leitmotivs you'll wish you'd never heard,
And a demented, shattering Cadenza.
I'm pained to say that scholarship insists
Cadenzas are conclusion to Concertos,
Not Sonatas—true Sonatas close
With what pedantic musicologists,
Waving their Ph.D.s beneath my nose,
Persist in calling Recapitulation.
My double ending is a Variation:
I couldn't choose between them once I chose
To write two endings, so, because I wrote a
Recapitulation and Cadenza,
My piece concludes two times—and then it ends
Again because I've added on a Coda.

To brush up on Sonata structure: first,
The Exposition sounds two melodies,
Deeply dissimilar, in different keys,
Major and minor. Part Two is a burst
Of brainstorms scholars call Development,
In which the two themes of the Exposition
Are changed and rearranged past recognition,
Distorted, fragmented, dissolved, and blent

Into chromatic superimposition,
Till, imperceptibly, two themes unite.
And then, if everything is going right,
The piece concludes in Recapitulation.

Exposition

Theme One: My life lacks what, in lacking you?
Theme Two: Does the material world exist?

(Ideally your neurons should resist,
As yet, connecting Numbers One and Two.
But note the skill, the frightening mastery,
The lunatic precision it entails
To merge these separate themes, the way train rails
Converge as they approach infinity.)

Development

I dreamed that an encyclopedia
Opened before my eyes and there I found
Analogies to sort of stack around
My what-is-life-without-you-here idea:

Like *nous* detached from Anaxagoras,
Like cosmic fire glimmering without
A Heraclitus there to find it out,
Like square roots waiting for Pythagoras,
Like One-ness riven from Parmenides,
Like Nothing without Gorgias to detect it,
Like paradox sans Zeno to perfect it,
Like plural worlds lacking Empedocles,
Like Plato's chairs and tables if you took
The furniture's Eternal Forms away,
Objects abandoned by Reality
Still look the same, but look the way things look
When I behold my life without you in it:
A screwy room where chairs and tables lack
Dimension from the front, the side, the back,
Like finity without the infinite,
Where tea parties are held without the Hatter,
It's like a single point withdrawn from Space,
It's like a physicist who cannot trace
The ultimate constituents of matter—

There is no evidence Matter exists.
Thus do I introduce Theme Number Two.
And I can't prove it, but I know it's true:
The physical eludes the physicists.
They've chased down matter past atomic rings
Into small shadows, and they've lost it there.
It seems that they can't find it anywhere.
They stalk imaginary floating things
Like amateurish lepidopterists
Round babbling brooks and mossy fairy knolls.
Their net strings map out squares of empty holes.
Behold them snatching something in their fists:
Their fingers uncurl, cautious, on the sight
Of Nothing crushed against the sweaty hand.
But then I'm prejudiced, you understand.
Not everyone on earth believes I'm right.
But lest you think I'm kidding, or perverse,
I went to hear a Lecture just last year
About some things which I hold very dear:
The smallest pieces of the universe.
The Lecturer referred to them as Quarks.
He seemed impervious to the mystery
Surrounding their invisibility.
I asked, when he concluded his remarks,
"But are Quarks physical?"
                              You'd think that he
Were someone nearly martyred and I'd said
Our duty's to die peacefully in bed.
He took his glasses off and blinked at me.

Were I John Milton, I would now destroy
This moment of high drama and deploy
A thirty-line Homeric simile.
But I'm not Milton, nor was meant to be.
He put his glasses on, and said, "Of course."

Now, I may be the south end of a horse,
But logically and analogically,
And physically, and metaphysically,
And, if it gets to that, religiously,
And absolutely scientifically,
I don't believe that Quarks can pass the test
Of Being There, and since they're fundamental,
Why, then, the world's a dream, and dreams are mental,
And since in mental matters East or West
I need you for this dream's interpretation—

Stop looking at your watch, for I've divined,
With these two themes uncomfortably combined,
It's time now for the Recapitulation.

Recapitulation

Frankly, I'm disinclined to reassert
The themes my Exposition indicated.
Stuffed-shirts there are, and hordes of overrated
Experts who would slay or badly hurt
With airy wave of hand my insights; no,
I will not play to them, I'll not rehash
My song though they with hard and cold cash
Should bribe me, or should tell me where to go.
My complex principles are explicated
Under "Development." So let them laugh:
I'll not permit this section to be half
So convoluted as anticipated.

Cadenza

Sing, Heav'nly Muse, and give me lyric flight,
Give me special effects, give me defiance
To challenge the Academy of Science
On fundamental points, and get them right;
Give me the strength to can the Latinisms,
To forge analogies between the thing
Nature abhors and my apartment; sing
To vanquish literary criticisms
If possible and literary sharks.
And even if you feel submicroscopic
Elements exceed me as a topic,
Please try to back me up regarding Quarks,
Thereby to advocate my metaphor
(Absence the vehicle, physics the tenor)
So that the Universal Void coincides
With showing—I daresay, with showing off—
The consequences of his going off;
By showing everything, in fact, but slides.

Coda

My heart detests, reviles, denounces, loathes
Your absence with a passion like a furnace.
The shirt of Love, said Eliot, will burn us;
And normally I'd add: "Love's other clothes
Burn just as badly," but good taste prevents
My introducing still another figure—
Good taste prevents this piece from getting bigger,
Lest theorists mark my brutish ignorance
Of Aristotle's golden-ruled proportion.
Line hundred forty-nine: to summarize,
Beginning with line hundred fifty-one,
How much it matters, love, that you come home—

But I've grown sensitive about this poem.
Its logic, its ideas, its sheer size
Were meant to buffalo and pulverize
Critical inquiries into its merit.
But I dislike it too; I too can't bear it;
I find it unendurably conceited,
Belligerent, high-handed, asinine;
I too can hardly force myself to read it;
Come home, before I write another line.

PAPER CITIES

The radio glimmers,
Cities alight in my room
Among cities of books
Stacked in towers.
Each book is a room. In one,
Flaubert affixes the date on the page, July,
And addresses the neglected Louise,
Advising his beauty by mail:
"Read, do not dream." Three months go by.
In my dictionary of saints,
One carries her torn breasts on a plate,
Another washes his severed head
In a fountain, others carry their cities
Before them on trays,
Like fragmented sets of chess.
Below, Gretel peers from a cage.
Above, Lear leans over his map
And chooses the liar;
I press my eyes,
I don't want to read.
But when I tire
Of making shadow-swans who make haste
In the radio light,
And arranging my hairpins in pentacles
And giant alphabets, I need other
Ways of wasting the night.

Through the doorway
The kitchen floor-squares make a chessboard

Whose figures have crumbled
To small heaps of dust.
It is morning for you where you sit
In the City of God,
Where every predicament, every desire
Possesses a saint intervening above it.
Saint Barbara, whose father instantly
Turned to a cinder that tangled
Into her broom,
Holds a stony tower
In the crook of one arm.
She presides over gunpowder
And those who die without rites.
You write in a room,
You write rather than dream,
The cities spring up from your pencil point,
Towers, chess, the captured queen
Over whose empty square you preside.
You press on your eyes
As if your head hurt, and the stars
With five points break apart
Into triangles whose corners are swept,
Bent, smoothed into circles
Rolling like wobbling zeroes away.
When you finally look up,
The day will be dark.
I draw crosses, chess,
Then affix names of streets to the lines,
A map, city squares.

When you touched my breasts I saw
Hand shadows, like bird inventions
By Arcimboldo the Marvelous,
Spring to the wall.
A room appeared when I kissed your face
Where with Yaasriel's seventy holy pencils
It is my duty everlastingly
To write your name, without looking up.
But the pencils roll and fall
From my desk in this rented place.
Louise touches the dreaming head
Of her daughter, but reads
The story aloud to the end
Where the bear comes back
And a lost girl has slept in his bed.
Upstairs my neighbors trace
Crossed lines above my head
In vanishing miles,
And I can't fix my eyes on the page
Where Flaubert writes that prose
Is a permanent rage,
Writes to Louise that he'll form
His book as a globe which will hang
"Suspended without visible support"
By the laws of style.
Rain hangs before my eyes
On the weather report.
Like continents beyond the windowsill

Clouds softly tear apart
As if a map were ripped to show
The world is hung on nothing,
He is right. Clouds sail past
The bent head of Louise as she writes back,
A message lost long since.
Countries break apart above the streets.
The window glitters black.
I touch my forehead to the glass.

Read, do not dream.
But my books are towers,
Rooms, dreams where the scenes tangle,
Visible through the stones.
A feather floats up from the page
Where the kitchen maid cries
As she plucks the weeping goose,
Or beats with a broom
White sheets into swans.
On the children-of-royalty's lawns
The beaten hoops stagger
Away from the merciless sticks.
And Lear sits in jail, cut to the brains.
He spreads his drenched map
And waits till it dries,
Then folds it into a pointed hat,
And the faded countries wave in his hair
Like tattered butterflies.

I cannot read,
But I sit at the base of the wall,
Wearing my hands for a hat.

Saint Clare possessed
Bilocal vision, which meant she could see
Events in places where she was not,
The way readers do.
It is morning for you.
You crouch behind your pencil.
If a rhythm branches through the forehead
Like the tree of which the empty page is made,
Gepetto appears with an ax.
He makes a child in which
The tree is hidden.
But Pinocchio's nose reverts
To a tree with leaves where the bird's egg
Rolls like a hoop from the nest and cracks
Into jagged triangles,
And little jaws open soundlessly.
I touch my head as if it were gashed,
Stories reel over the wires,
Narratives when I desire
All things to stare blankly back.

In the hollow squares I write,
"I envy the unfaithful."
They know what to do with the night.
Then I draw the pentacle,

The star they call the endless knot
Because in drawing it the pencil point
Is never lifted once.
The star with five points,
The five paper hats,
A starry crown of triangles
For the betrayed.
And I stare at what I have done,
Beholding in fright
What I have made,

A pyramid wreath, a city of tombs,
And Flaubert writes, "Books grow huge
Like pyramids, and in the end
They almost frighten you."
Louise crumples this into a ball,
And I put my pencil down.
The dust on the kitchen floor:
Crumbled towers, the dust of a vanished crown
In the empty square of the queen.
Upstairs my neighbors pace
And the rain flies down.
Saints look down from the towers
That rise from the paper you spread
Like a map where you write
And do not look up.
I lay the broom in my lap
Like the grizzled head of a saint
With a string for a crown.

Louise pins flowers on her hat
And bursts in on Flaubert.
From the dusty straws,
Like a feather a dead moth floats up
Which I pluck from the air
To set down on the page
Where the words came on
And the lines crossed, streets, city squares
Near the crumpled paper and tower of dreams.
The moth's tiny wrecked skull, its rumpled face
Preside weightless, hushed
Over paper cities:
Little one, in whose papery jaws,
As it is written on paper,
The world is crushed.

SNOW MELTING

Snow melting when I left you, and I took
This fragile bone we'd found in melting snow
Before I left, exposed beside a brook
Where raccoons washed their hands. And this, I know,

Is that raccoon we'd watched for every day.
Though at the time her wild human hand
Had gestured inexplicably, I say
Her meaning now is more than I can stand.

We've reasons, we have reasons, so we say,
For giving love, and for withholding it.
I who would love must marvel at the way
I know aloneness when I'm holding it,

Know near and far as words for live and die,
Know distance, as I'm trying to draw near,
Growing immense, and know, but don't know why,
Things seen up close enlarge, then disappear.

Tonight this small room seems too huge to cross.
And my life is that looming kind of place.
Here, left with this alone, and at a loss
I hold an alien and vacant face

Which shrinks away, and yet is magnified—
More so than I seem able to explain.
Tonight the giant galaxies outside
Are tiny, tiny on my windowpane.

IV

THE HEAVENLY FEAST

Simone Weil, 1909–1943

Only the stones at first
Seem to have a part in this,
And the little height of the grass
As it gains a fraction-inch

By gripping the shallow soil
With all the shocking might
Of hunger and of thirst,
As if the soil itself

Were all that's left on earth.
I think the grass alone
Can hold within its grasp
What matters to it most,

And still it looks bereft,
And famished as the stones.
I watch a stream of moths
Proceeding on their ways,

They carve out tortuous paths
As if they were intent
On entering unseen
And ever-smaller doors.

So four years into the war,
And cut off from the ones
Whose circumstance you felt
And suffering as yours,

You carved yourself a path
Through ever-narrowing doors
Of hunger and of thirst,
And entered them day by day,

Refusing all at first
But that ration of food
Your people could obtain
Behind the lines in France,

And then refusing that,
From summer into fall
You cut your ration back
To send your part to them,

Your part diminishing
To rations cut in half
And cut in half again,
And then nothing at all

But water at the last
Sipped for the nurse's sake,
You finally lacked the strength
Even to lift your hands:

Father, I cannot stand
To think of them and eat.
Send it to them, it is theirs.
Send this food for them,

For my people still in France.
And turned your face away,
As famished as the grass.
Only the stones at first

Seem to have a part in this,
And the little height of the grass
As it gains a fraction-inch.
But hidden in the grass

As if the grass itself
Were giving out a cry,
I overhear the finch
Begin her native rhyme

And toil to paraphrase
Her version of your words.
It seems she tries and tries
Until the words come clear,

It is theirs, she seems to say,
Or that is what I hear,
And again: It is theirs, it is theirs.
And the plover joins in praise

With her fluttering, murmured prayers:
Send it to them, it is theirs.
And the blackbirds breaking wide
Take it up in their dialects

To sing you in their way,
I swear I can hear the words,
Send it to them, they say,
Send it to them, it is theirs,

Then all the birds of the air
Give thanks above your grave,
As if they were your cause
And those you meant to save,

As if the birds were there
In attendance at the end,
And, seeing the sacrifice
Had borne your body up,

So wasted as it was,
To your chair in Paradise,
And saw, before they fled,
Your first breathtaking act

Before the heavenly feast,
The bread set at your place:
To refuse to eat till none
On earth has less than you,

Though God in pity take
Your hands and lift them toward
His table for your sake.
Father, they have no food,

Send it to them, it is theirs.
And the birds returning here
Give tongue to what they've heard,
They tell the grass and stones

And the stream of moths who carve
Their tortuous paths in the air.
But how in giving thanks
Can we calculate the worth

Of one who chose to starve?
You held within your grasp
Our hunger and our thirst.
And the little height of the grass

As it gains a fraction-inch
Seems to have a part in this.
It grips with a shocking might
What matters to the last,

As if the soil itself
Were all that's left on earth,
And all the earth were held
Within its famished grasp.

ADVENT CALENDAR

Bethlehem in Germany,
Glitter on the sloping roofs,
Breadcrumbs on the windowsills,
Candles in the Christmas trees,
Hearths with pairs of empty shoes:
Panels of Nativity
Open paper scenes where doors
Open into other scenes,
Some recounted, some foretold.
Blizzard-sprinkled flakes of gold
Gleam from small interiors,
Picture-boxes in the stars
Open up like cupboard doors
In a cabinet Jesus built.

Southern German villagers,
Peasants in the mica frost,
See the comet streaming down,
Heavenly faces, each alone,
Faces lifted, startled, lost,
As if lightning lit the town.

Sitting in an upstairs window
Patiently the village scholar
Raises his nearsighted face,
Interrupted by the star.
Left and right his hands lie stricken
Useless on his heavy book.
When I lift the paper door

In the ceiling of his study
One canary-angel glimmers,
Flitting in the candelabra,
Peers and quizzes him: Rabbi,
What are the spheres surmounted by?
But his lips are motionless.
Child, what are you asking for?
Look, he gazes past the roofs,
Gazes where the bitter North,
Stretched across the empty place,
Opens door by door by door.

This is childhood's shrunken door.
When I touch the glittering crumbs,
When I cry to be admitted,
No one answers, no one comes.

And the tailor's needle flashes
In mid-air with thread pulled tight,
Stitching a baptismal gown.
But the gown, the seventh door,
Turns up an interior
Hidden from the tailor's eyes:
Baby presents like the boxes
Angels hold on streets and stairways,
Wooden soldier, wooden sword,
Chocolate coins in crinkled gold,
Hints of something bought and sold,
Hints of murder in the stars.

Baby's gown is sown with glitter
Spread across the tailor's lap.
Up above his painted ceiling
Baby mouse's skeleton
Crumbles in the mouse's trap.

Leaning from the cliff of heaven,
Indicating whom he weeps for,
Joseph lifts his lamp above
The infant like a candle-crown.
Let my fingers touch the silence
Where the infant's father cries.
Give me entrance to the village
From my childhood where the doorways
Open pictures in the skies.
But when all the doors are open,
No one sees that I've returned.
When I cry to be admitted,
No one answers, no one comes.
Clinging to my fingers only
Pain, like glitter bits adhering,
When I touch the shining crumbs.

SUPERNATURAL LOVE

My father at the dictionary-stand
Touches the page to fully understand
The lamplit answer, tilting in his hand

His slowly scanning magnifying lens,
A blurry, glistening circle he suspends
Above the word "Carnation." Then he bends

So near his eyes are magnified and blurred,
One finger on the miniature word,
As if he touched a single key and heard

A distant, plucked, infinitesimal string,
"The obligation due to every thing
That's smaller than the universe." I bring

My sewing needle close enough that I
Can watch my father through the needle's eye,
As through a lens ground for a butterfly

Who peers down flower-hallways toward a room
Shadowed and fathomed as this study's gloom
Where, as a scholar bends above a tomb

To read what's buried there, he bends to pore
Over the Latin blossom. I am four,
I spill my pins and needles on the floor

Trying to stitch "Beloved" X by X.
My dangerous, bright needle's point connects
Myself illiterate to this perfect text

I cannot read. My father puzzles why
It is my habit to identify
Carnations as "Christ's flowers," knowing I

Can give no explanation but "Because."
Word-roots blossom in speechless messages
The way the thread behind my sampler does

Where following each X I awkward move
My needle through the word whose root is love.
He reads, "A pink variety of Clove,

Carnatio, the Latin, meaning flesh."
As if the bud's essential oils brush
Christ's fragrance through the room, the iron-fresh

Odor carnations have floats up to me,
A drifted, secret, bitter ecstasy,
The stems squeak in my scissors, *Child, it's me,*

He turns the page to "Clove" and reads aloud:
"The clove, a spice, dried from a flower-bud."
Then twice, as if he hasn't understood,

He reads, "From French, for *clou*, meaning a nail."
He gazes, motionless. "Meaning a nail."
The incarnation blossoms, flesh and nail,

I twist my threads like stems into a knot
And smooth "Beloved," but my needle caught
Within the threads, *Thy blood so dearly bought,*

The needle strikes my finger to the bone.
I lift my hand, it is myself I've sewn,
The flesh laid bare, the threads of blood my own,

I lift my hand in startled agony
And call upon his name, "Daddy daddy"—
My father's hand touches the injury

As lightly as he touched the page before,
Where incarnation bloomed from roots that bore
The flowers I called Christ's when I was four.

NOTES

Kremlin of Smoke

The twenty-year-old Chopin was visiting Stuttgart when he heard that Warsaw had fallen to the Russians; his journal entry for that night accuses God of being a Russian. Chopin never returned to Warsaw.

Several details in this fictional portrait, such as Chopin's gift for mimicry, his mother's love of Rousseau, and the eccentric dress of his childhood piano teacher, are drawn from Chopin's letters and journals and from Adam Zamoyski's biography, *Chopin*.

The Self-Portrait of Ivan Generalić

Generalić addresses his wife, who had died in the same year that he painted this self-portrait.

Imaginary Prisons

The title is a translation of *Carceri d'Invenzione*, G. Battista Piranesi's series of engravings of fantastical prisons, which was published in Rome *c.* 1760.

The Heavenly Feast

Simone Weil died in August 1943, in a sanatorium in Ashford, Kent, England. Several years after her death, an epitaph in Italian was placed anonymously on her grave. It translates: "My solitude has held in its grasp the grief of others until my death."